The Real Yoga: Life
By D'ana Baptiste

DEDICATION

I dedicate this book to the people of Yelapa, whom I love with all my heart. I can't wait until I'm there again. To Flor, Hector, Ismael, César, Fatima, Terésa, Fabiola, Rodolpho, Rafa, Michel, and the staff at Los Naranjos, Casa Perico and El Jardin.

Space Between

"The only way that we can live, is if we grow. The only way that we can grow is if we change. The only way that we can change is if we learn. The only way we can learn is if we are exposed. And the only way that we can become exposed is if we throw ourselves out into the open. Do it. Throw yourself."~C. Joy Bell

I feel helpless. Gutted. No phone conversation or in person exchange could ever, ever, get to the root of how I feel. Processing this abandonment will have to be done alone.

For the first time since I started my working life, I am not running a business and have no clue what job I'll have next. I'm in a tunnel - the space between- a space created by default. On my 50th birthday, my business, my livelihood – what and who I was in the world - was ripped violently and suddenly away from me by people I loved and trusted.

The wave of nauseating social media filled with lies and misrepresentations and hatred began to truly crush me. The vapid emojis, hollow one-liners and patronizing well-intentioned memes didn't really help me feel any better. In fact, I felt guilty about not feeling better. I realized that moving through this "space" would have to be done outside of the realms of social media.

Life has stopped. I am swallowed whole. I've disappeared into the belly of the whale. No breath, no light, no air, no reprieve.

While I was busy cleaning up the mess of what had happened, I mistakenly thought my pain was just boxed up all neat and tidy; something I could store in my attic and forget about.
But that's not how this works. Contrary to popular belief and a culture that perpetuates numbness — I can't move it or shake it or drink it or chase it or throw it or bury it. The only way out is through.

I chose to retreat to Yelapa, Mexico to move through it. To feel and write and cry and sleep and walk and swim myself, breath by breath, out of the well of grief I in which I was submerged, out of the public eye.

These are my musings, the lessons I slowly learned from the people and the place that is Yelapa. These writings are how I renegotiated my relationship with Yoga. These entries are my way of coming back to myself.

Falling

I finally figured out that not every crisis can be managed. As much as we want to keep ourselves safe, we can't protect ourselves from everything. If we want to embrace life, we also have to embrace chaos." ~Susan Elizabeth Phillips, Breathing Room

The only way to get to Yelapa is on a water taxi, after flying into Puerto Vallarta. You can also travel around their small bay by water taxi, if you decide you don't want to walk through the pueblo. There are no cars and no roads in Yelapa!

Water taxis are not only a great way to travel, they also provide entertainment value. Especially when full of tourists. Part of my daily routine at the beach is to watch the travelers disembark the boat after it pulls up on the beach. One thing you can count on is that at least one person will fall into the surf, get wet, lose their flip-flops, soak their beach towel, watch their sunglasses drift away, or get stuck in a spontaneous yoga pose halfway in the water.

What's amazing about this process is that everyone is smiling, laughing, and even posing as they attempt to get out of this boat "safely." Back in the USA, if we fell while trying to exit a boat, we'd be furiously blaming and taking legal action, vowing to get even with the company who dared to get our feet wet.

We'd demand safety measures, outfit everyone with a life jacket and helmet, hire people to escort everyone safely off the boat, and petition for new laws against allowing companies to put people in such danger.

Here in Mexico though, getting out of the water taxi becomes a part of the adventure. An immersion into a culture that does not provide safety rails. Here, we fall from the boat on our asses, in front of a beach full of people. Here, rather than getting embarrassed, we laugh along with the spectators and actually . . . have fun.

We have fun falling. We laugh as we watch our flip flops washing down the shore. We wave at the people on the beach laughing with us. We acknowledge our klutziness as we realize we're entirely okay.

Maybe we are all craving a respite from surety. A rest from our guardrails and safety rules. Maybe we crave an opportunity to fall, even to be seen falling. Maybe we need a reminder that even when (or if) we scrape a knee or bruise a butt cheek, we're alive.

We're living. We're falling. And we love it.

Thoughts Upon Waking

The Thing Is
to love life, to love it even
when you have no stomach for it
and everything you've held dear
crumbles like burnt paper in your hands,
your throat filled with the silt of it.
When grief sits with you, its tropical heat
thickening the air, heavy as water
more fit for gills than lungs;
when grief weights you like your own flesh
only more of it, an obesity of grief,
you think, How can a body withstand this?
Then you hold life like a face
between your palms, a plain face,
no charming smile, no violet eyes,
and you say, yes, I will take you
I will love you, again.
~ Ellen Bass

So here I am, crushed and annihilated and
heartbroken. Alone in Mexico.

I wish I could hire a doctor to surgically remove the
heaviness. I wish I could lift it or hold it or throw it
into the sea. I wish there were a shortcut to send these
feelings off into the stars where I never have to see
them or feel them again. But I can't get rid of any of it.

I wake up to the memory of the thirteen people who, a year ago, began planning to steal my business from me. In a series of secret meetings and with a lot of pressure and monetary reward promised, the instigator of this devious plan convinced two thirds of my staff, men and women I felt were my family, to stab me in the back. They agreed, because if they didn't all do it then no one would get the financial reward to help her steal my yoga studio right out from under me. My life's work.

They staged a "lock out" on my fiftieth birthday so they could spread the lie that a beloved studio that had served the community for 12 years had closed for good. They believed I would go under within a few days, without enough teachers and support staff.

They encouraged the community to stop supporting not only me but all of the instructors who chose to stay. They systematically spread egregious lies, telling students I'd gambled the payroll away, or didn't pay them, or that I was an alcoholic, or that I was losing my mind. They defended their very non-yogic actions by claiming they were doing this for me because they loved me.

I was publicly humiliated. My integrity was impugned; my reputation slandered. It was particularly unfathomable and shocking because the people who set out to destroy everything I had invested in for the last twelve years of my life were the very same people I thought of as family.

People who'd celebrated my birthday with me a week before the planned walkout. Danced with me. Hugged me. Laughed with me.

I wake up every morning wondering how they spent time with me without giving away what they were about to do. Long time students/friends/colleagues I'd gone out of my way to support and accept; I called them all family. I never saw it coming.

I wake here every morning wondering what I did to warrant this level of betrayal. And then I move from wondering to intense waves of self-doubt. I doubt my ability to be in this world. I feel stupid. I feel worthless. I feel expendable; wadded up and thrown away.

All of this remembering occurs before I open my eyes. I force myself to notice where I'm at today.

The ocean is there for me. She's constant, she's real, and she's inviting me into her warm embrace. A quick swim will do me good, so I run down the stairs to the water, and dive in.

Eyes Wide Open

"He wished for solitude and for the comfort of knowing that his life depended not on the multitude but on remaining himself."
~Colm Toibin (from *The Master*)

Solitude. I've been taught in yoga that the only way to experience it is to close my eyes, close my doors, and close out the world. But the solitude I'm discovering these days is one I can experience with eyes open. People around. Sounds, smells, tastes, and feels have become my cocoon.

Stillness and solitude exist in the spaces between the noise of the squawking chichilacas and pounding surf. Surrounded by people (even crowds), I realize that solitude and solidarity exist together; one doesn't negate the other. The world doesn't have to be a place I lose myself; it offers me every opportunity to remain myself.

This is the real yoga. The realization that the world is meant to be alive in. The deep and urgent prompting to look for myself in the ocean, the trees, the birds, the wind, the stars, the sand, and the silence. I'm done closing my eyes.

14

Books

The truth of wise teachers and great books are gifts. The truth you discover through reason is a treasure. The most rare and precious jewel is the truth born of experience. Experience your true self and become truth itself. The maps and travelogues left behind by others are great blessings, full of useful information and inspiration, but they cannot take the journey for us. When it is time to merge onto the highway or pull up anchor, we are ostensibly on our own.
~Sutra 1:49, Yoga Sutras of Patanjali

I brought a stack of books with me; reading is one of my favorite activities and when my world turned upside down, I stopped reading. So I bring a book to the beach and usually read one book each day. It's another thing I can do to come back to myself. To whom I've always been. However, when I find myself on the last page, once again I'm left with my thoughts, my feelings, and the overwhelm of being lost.

I want to feel all of this so I can move through it; putting it off until I finish my book is my avoidance mechanism of choice. But the feelings come flooding back now.

Their plan was to move back into the same building, sign the lease out from under me, bring back the same staff, and leave me with nothing. Their instigator pretended for 6 months to be in negotiation with me to buy my business. This gave her access to all of my financial records, the database, the business protocols.

The studio manager spent countless hours with her while I was constantly meeting with her "partner in crime," because we wanted a smooth and caring transition, both for the yoga students and for the yoga teachers.

Even those meetings were to be used against me as evidence that I was not around. They purposely arranged meetings outside of the studio, kept me there for hours, or canceled last minute. I kept trusting them because I trusted that we all wanted a smooth transition.

I didn't know who her "secret" investor was at the time, only finding out later that he was funding a hostile takeover, not a legitimate buy out, doing it for personal reasons to "take me down" because I'd refused to let him work for me.

I sit and look at the surf washing lightly on the sand and wonder how I missed it. I feel heavy; I want to hide, to disappear. I look at the water and imagine these dark and dreary sensations drawing me under.

I jump into the ocean, ready to drown, only to feel lifted and light, floating on my back, out into the bay, seeing the sun with new eyes, my salty tears mixing with the salt of the sea.

And I feel. I don't feel better, but I have the courage to keep feeling. Or at least reading. And that's something.

Moon

I want to write about faith,
about the way the moon rises
over cold snow, night after night,
faithful even as it fades from fullness,
slowly becoming that last curving and impossible
sliver of light before the final darkness.
But I have no faith myself
I refuse it even the smallest entry.
Let this then, my small poem,
like a new moon, slender and barely open,
be the first prayer that opens me to faith.
~David Whyte

Tonight, as I walked home, there was no moonlight to
light my way; no moon to find in the sky. It was dark
and I was alone, feeling scared of the dark in the same
way I felt as a child looking out the window on those
moonless nights. I didn't know when I was a girl that
the moon never really disappears; she's always there
but sometimes she is hidden from view.

Just as I fear the darkness of a moonless night, I avoid
the darkest corners of who I am. I don't want to admit
that I'm hurt, that I'm lost, that I can't see the pathway
home. But I know that tomorrow I'll find a sliver of
light again, and this light will grow stronger as it
always does.

The moon reminds me that it is whole even when it is hidden in complete darkness. I too, am whole, even though I feel enveloped in my brokenness.

The moon reminds me of how all aspects of myself are worthy and valid of my attention. Waxing or waning, new or full, the moon is always a perfect moon.

Sleep

"She felt around herself for her true perfect name and though it took a long and lonesome moment, finally she felt it there. It was shivery and scant. Scared. Skint. But just around the edges it was still scintillant. It was still hers. It shone."
~Patrick Rothfuss, *The Slow Regard of Silent Things*

Tonight, I feel a palpable sense of peace and security as I prepare to sleep alone in my open palapa. I feel "safe," even in the knowledge my heart is truly broken; sometimes I feel the sharp edges in my dreams. While the initial splintering occurred in an instant (followed by a spectacular and very public free fall) I spent six months scrambling for footing that continued to crumble like sand. I lost my foundation. I lost peace of mind. I lost my name. And I lost a lot of sleep.

When it first happened, I woke myself crying every night for months, becoming so accustomed to my eyes leaking that eventually I slept through it, only to wake to the evidence of dried salt on damp pillows.

Here in Mexico though, I'm sleeping through most nights. My nightly ritual is to say goodnight to the moon and the stars, put the extra blanket on my bed, and climb under the covers.

The waves lull me to sleep as soon as I settle in with my book. The sound of the ocean roars into the open space, washing away any potential "review" of the past. My mind settles into silence, and in that space right before sleep, I find my name. My perfect and true remembrance of me is allowed here.

As I sleep, rolling over into another shattered piece of my soul, I am comforted by the salty, thick, night air and the Mexican blanket that I've come to believe has love woven into it.

No Walls

"Those who contemplate the beauty of the earth find reserves of strength that will endure as long as life lasts. There is something infinitely healing in the repeated refrains of nature — the assurance that dawn comes after night, and spring after winter."
~ Rachel Carson

A palapa is what people live in here in Yelapa. Open air "casas" without walls. The ocean crashes right at the foot of this palapa. The ocean breeze keeps the mosquitoes from congregating. The sun gently coaxes me awake.

It's cold every morning, refreshing as I face another day of heat, so I wrap myself up in my beach blanket, snuggle up to my coffee cup, stare out into the abyss that is mama ocean, and an hour goes by.

This is my new way of practicing presence. I keep my eyes open to watch the pelicans dive, the magnificent frigates (and they are magnificent) hovering, the shimmering sardines jumping out of the sea to paint the surface silver.

I wait for whales and dolphins to surface and play. To see a whale breach, to hear the sound of a huge tailfin slapping the sea's surface. To witness the grace of dolphins as they traverse the bay. To feel completely connected. I can't miss experiencing the world when there are no walls to block it.

Tree

Ah listen, for silence is not lonely!
Imitate the magnificent trees
That speak no word of their rapture, but only
Breathe largely the luminous breeze.
~From *Corot* by D.H. Lawrence

Today I walked to the small fresh water pool right in the heart of the pueblo, or town, of Yelapa. It's a short walk uphill with a reward at the end of a beautiful waterfall and fresh coconut water for 10 pesos. (You can also add tequila or rum to the coco water, should you desire)!

A tree stopped me in my tracks, so unusual and unique, so daunting and yet so unassuming. How many times had I walked past this tree without noticing it? How many other people walk by without seeing it? I wonder how the tree feels, going largely unnoticed and unappreciated.

Because my destination was the fresh water pool, and my anticipation was that refreshing swim, I wasn't open to the beauty of this tree. I couldn't hear the call, a whisper really, because my mind was full of thoughts of the fresh coconut awaiting me, or keeping the pace of the hike going, or how hot it was and how I couldn't wait to dive into the cold fresh water.

I've missed out on so many quiet promptings by hustling toward ultimate destinations.

Missing - and now missing no longer - this tree, I learned today that it is time to tune into the whispers of my environment as I progress more intimately in my life. Practice tuning in to what is right in front of me, because that is the only thing that is real and is all I need to feed my soul.

Pie

An appreciative heart empowers food to open its treasures to you — to the degree that you are willing to open your heart to the silent message in your meals. When we approach food with loving intention, we go beyond mindfulness to regard the sacred connection between food, nature, and humankind. Such deeply felt thankfulness for food and all other gifts bestowed by our creator is what connects us to the origin of and the force that creates food. To care in such a way is inherently other-oriented because instead of focusing on your own food related concerns, you are paying attention to the food before you, regarding the mystery of life of life it contains and provides.
~Nischala Devi, *The Healing Power of Yoga*

I've started to consistently live in this different reality of "you don't know if you'll ever get to experience this again" mentality. It's why I dive into the waterfall rather than simply observe its majesty. Why I kayak by myself even though it scares me. Why I don't mind living with lizards. And it's why I eat pie on the beach. Yes, pie on the beach. Warm, freshly baked, lovingly offered, pie from the famous pie lady of Yelapa.

She and her family walk the beach, tupperware containers full of warm pie balanced on their heads, offering the ultimate decadence to us tourists in our chaises. Those of us who come to this beach to eat fresh fish and guacamole return again and again for the pie.

Since she sells eight flavors (apple, banana, cheese, chocolate, chocolate coconut, coconut, pecan, and lemon meringue), I of course indulge every day. I can't say I didn't gain any weight, only that the weight I did gain was well worth it.

She's not going to be around forever and I may never make it back to Yelapa, so I'm going to keep enjoying these tastes of heaven for the present moment.

Community

So don't be frightened, dear friend, if a sadness confronts
you larger than any you have ever known, casting its
shadow over all you do. You must think that something is
happening within you, and remember that life has not
forgotten you; it holds you in its hand and will not let you
fall. Why would you want to exclude from your life any
uneasiness, any pain, any depression, since you don't know
what work they are accomplishing within.
~Ranier Maria Rilke

How do I describe the people of Yelapa? With warm
hugs and daily "hola" or "buenas dias" greetings, I
quickly get to know this small community after my
years of visiting. To be welcomed by name; to see a
face light up when I walk into their "tienda," to have a
store owner tell me "for you it's free," means
everything. It's such a small yet friendly village that
it's easy to spend at least an hour greeting each other
as we walk down the one path through town.

At "home" after my initial shock, I felt the same
connection; a rallying around me that saved me and
saved my belief in humanity. An entire community
came together. Even when I was the only one teaching
all day or when a completely unknown teacher
showed up to teach, enough students continued to
attend classes. They stayed through the stress,
attended subbed classes, or took yet another class
from me. People showed up at a time when they were
giving more than they were getting.

Teachers continued to show up to teach even in the midst of uncertainty, not really knowing if I'd be able to keep the doors open, but showing up anyway. Pressured to answer questions they had no answer for. Sending me love and support without getting anything in return. Conducting themselves with professionalism and poise. Without them I would have lost all hope.

Other "competing" studio owners stepped right in to help me. They came over to teach classes (for free) and take classes; they sent staff members to cover part of the schedule so I wasn't teaching twelve times a day. Studio owners who made me sit outside in the sun, held me tight and let me cry in their arms, took me for walks, bought me dinner. Studio owners who could have celebrated my downfall chose instead to make sure I never felt alone, and make sure the studio survived.

Our reception staff chose to stay, even though they took the bulk of the anger from the students who just wanted to come and take a class at their neighborhood studio without drama.

My landlord and her husband were the first to alert me to their true intent. They stood in the way of the first attempt at a hostile takeover, and the first to declare publicly that they stood with me.

My boys took care of so much when all I had time to do was take care of keeping the studio open. They, along with their friends, took care of the dog, the house, the yard, the errands, the groceries, and me. I was never home. I rarely saw my sons for the rest of the summer.

And finally, new owners, who knew this was a sinking ship, came in to rescue the studio. With all of that help and support I survived. Barely.

Sensing

What I sense when I sense

Frigate playing
Sailboat resting
Sunrise dousing
Pelican waiting

Palm tree breathing
Crabs skittering
Ocean speaking
Coastline answering

Wind caressing
Light embracing
Sun warming
Sand grounding

Salt

Door

*"We keep moving forward, opening new doors and doing
new things, because we're curious and curiosity keeps
leading us down new paths."*
~Walt Disney

I spent the day in Puerto Vallarta today. Started to
notice the way every door seems to have its own
personality. Lack of uniformity here leads to quiet
expressions of singularity. The buildings themselves
seem to exude an interesting history; an invitation to
step through the door and find out what awaits me.

People leave their doors open more often than not,
and tend to hang out in their doorways, beckoning my
gaze toward their open door, welcoming a glimpse
into their transparent lives. I notice how people here
aren't putting on any act. Their smiles are real and
their laughter, genuine. Their willingness to include
me makes me want to know them better, each of them
in their own unique way.

As I walk through the neighborhoods here it dawns
on me that it's not complex understanding I crave, it's
simple connection. I love being in the presence of
someone who isn't trying to sort me out, define me, or
best me. I love experiencing the shy wave from the old
man smoking his cigar, the playful "hola" from the
little girl on the sidewalk, the quick story from the
shopkeeper selling me a fan.

The interest they show me makes me feel like I matter to them. People here seem simple only because they lack pretense.

I believe a lot of Americans see this culture in a one dimensional way; dismissing it as "too simplistic" as if there's nothing to learn here. As if we are still missionaries out to bring all of our knowledge and superiority to them, these "simple" people. But here, even the doors prove that theory wrong.

Beasts of Burden

What we call a self is actually a story about our experience of life. And we construct the story because we're trying to give some order to what is actually a remarkably chaotic process. And then we get seduced by the seeming consistency of the story that we've constructed. And now, instead of just relating directly to our experience, we relate to our experience in terms of the story, and that's where the difficulties start.
~Ken McLeod

The sound of horses' hooves on the rocks below the casa brings me back to what's happening right now. I look to see these reliable beasts traversing the rocks, as they do every day.

I want not to feel sorry for these animals that carry loads of food and building supplies all day long, back and forth, up and down this path. When I hear their hoof beats it pains me a little. The horseshoes scraping the pathway grate on my nerves and for a moment I want to be the activist that fights for the mules' lives. I want to enforce my standards on this culture.

And then I remember it's also what I love about Yelapa. There are no cars, no trucks, no traffic here. A few all terrain vehicles drive the path once in a while delivering goods to the stores and the bars, but most everyone walks everywhere and carries supplies by boat or by horse/mule/donkey.

I get to see my mind wrestling with my desire to protect animals and my belief that I love this town. I get to notice that I am once again imposing my sense of superiority on a culture I say that I honor. I'm inserting my story and my feelings of being misused into this experience.

It's another great lesson in presence. We all have the capacity to see how our minds work; to realize our own inconsistencies and biases. To see with an unclouded mind how sometimes we aren't exactly the way we think we are.

Today I'll follow the donkeys, horses, and mules loaded down with boxes all the way to the point to see where they go all day. I'll walk along with them with only the desire to learn from another culture.

The Remedy

Don't run away from grief, o soul
Look for the remedy inside the pain.
Because the rose came from the thorn
and the ruby came from a stone.
~ Rumi

And yes you could say I was strong. But after being at the studio all day everyday, I'd go home and collapse. Cry myself to sleep. Wake myself screaming and crying. I wanted to die. I prayed that God would just make my kidneys fail or something so that at least my sons would have my life insurance. I was maxed out in every way you can be maxed out. I had nothing to give except my teaching.

My heart broke into at least a hundred pieces. I was informed daily of the lies circulating about me, of the students who'd believed the lies, of long time attendees who'd followed them, about who financed the entire fallout. Every single day I showed up with all of the courage I could muster. But inside I felt like a tiny bird with a broken wing.

I came to Mexico in a state of complete distrust. I lost an entire piece of myself the day I realized that people hated me while pretending to love me. I had seen these people almost daily for 12 years but had never really seen them for who they truly are. I've never been more surprised and shocked. I'm still incredulous. I did NOT see this coming.

Here in my open air palapa, neighbors at the next
property can see me and I can see them. We've been
observing each other observe the ocean for hours. We
acknowledge each other from afar; wave and smile.
We drink our coffee together yet apart.
Later, we'll walk by each other on the path and say
"Hola." We know each other without small talk. We
get each other.

They do their yoga. I watch them do their yoga and
want to feel like doing yoga too. But I don't. I don't
feel like it. I don't do it. I no longer trust yoga. It
dawns on me that this, even this fear, this distrust, this
lack and this isolation is all I can do and be right now.
The peace I feel from this is enough. I needed a break.
I need a break. The break from yoga is my remedy.

"I will be okay. Just not today."
~ unknown

Shells

We are like seashells upon the beach:
beautiful and unique,
each with a story to tell.
~ unknown

On the weekends or after 2 pm every afternoon,
children from age 4 – 10 will walk around holding a
cardboard box full of shells.

"Compra?" they ask everyone on their chaises
longues. "No, gracias," says almost everyone.

All these Americanized thoughts flood in, because
what I see first is children who are "overworked." I
see people who won't give a kid a dollar. I curse the
parents for making their kids go out and sell shells on
the beach. I want them to have time to "just be a kid."
So I "do my part" and call them over.

They spend a lot of time arguing with me whether I
hold out a ten peso coin or a 50 peso bill. They push
for more and I push for less. This is expected; the
children enjoy it and get to practice their business
skills. Many times, when I offer "too little," the kid
will walk away, rolling his or her eyes, losing patience
with my bargaining.

And that's when I notice that these kids aren't
overworked and underfed. They're having a good
time, honing functional life skills.

Interacting with people from all over the world with no fear, no apology, and no bullshit. Understanding that they'll hear "no" many times before they hear a "yes."

These kids are their own boss, entrepreneurs who, after an hour, will go home to play with their siblings or practice their dancing or do their homework.

When I was their age, I'd spend summer and fall selling vegetables door to door. Vegetables I grew in my own plot of land. I'd drag my wagon full of zucchini, tomatoes, beans, peas, potatoes, radishes, and later pumpkins through my neighborhood. Each neighbor who took pity on me got me one step closer to an empty wagon.

In the winter and spring I would use the money earned from selling vegetables to pay for candy to sell from a stand we'd set up outside each Saturday as we saw kids walking, skating, riding or sledding by.

These kids selling shells on the beach remind me of those early days when I was learning about business. Starting a business, running a business, re-investing in a business, creating multiple streams of income, and hard work. I never felt picked on--except those early mornings I had to wake up before sunrise to go weed my portion of the garden! The skills I learned from selling my wares those many years ago still inform me today.

I've gotten to know them now, so feel comfortable asking these beautiful children what they will do with their money. The older kids are saving for school uniforms or dance costumes. The younger kids just smile at me and shrug their shoulders and say "maybe a Fanta."

They feel no shame in walking the beach selling shells. They are proud of the work they do and the pesos they earn. And I can't wait to interact with them again tomorrow.

Sounding Time

"Part of doing something is listening.
We are listening.
To the sun. To the stars. To the wind."
~Madeleine L'Engle, *Swiftly Tilting Planet*

Water Taxis bounce over the sea this morning to wake me. I realize it's 7:30; the first taxi of the day is headed out from the pier. The sky is still dark. Every day there's difference in where and when the sun shows herself. A natural, non-fabricated change that introduces difference softly, reassuringly, not harshly.

I roll over to wake and feel the salty thick air move through the mosquito net. With no TV and spotty internet, the sunrise becomes a major attraction, one I don't want to miss.

Wrapped in my warm blanket, coffee in hand, I watch, I listen, I feel, and begin writing.

It's cold today. My hands keep cramping up. Small snails have appeared on the rocks along the shore. Jellyfish are visible in the gray sea; billowy clouds cover the sky.

The rhythm of the horses, mules, and donkeys carrying their workload is the perfect backdrop for my musings.

It's 8:30 am now, and I know this because the water taxi is stopping to pick up from Playa Isabel, a small beach just steps away from my casa. People bound for Puerto Vallarta jump in, braving the surf, because everyone gets their feet wet getting into and out of the water taxi. It's an adventure I've loved from the first time I had to do it.

I can now differentiate other sounds. I can tell when a water taxi bounces past, or when a fishing boat slowly floats by.

The sound of the surf on the rocks changes at low or high tide. The intensity of the crashing high tide is easy to hear.

The ocean doesn't drown out the songs of the parakeets, the arguments of the crows, and the remarks of the jays but by this time of the morning the birds are quiet. The seagulls, however, squawk all day long. A heavenly sound; one I've grown to embrace. The turkey vultures, perched on top of black rocks, have full conversations.

My mind is full of wonderings now. I wonder if Pelicans make a sound. I don't want to google the answer. It's not about knowing the answer. It's about letting myself stay in wonder.

Curiosity feels good to me, so I let it lead me for a while. Having no answers empowers me somehow.

When people ask me what I do, who I am, where I am going next, I feel pressured to offer an appropriate answer. The answer of a 50 year old. A responsible adult. But I was a responsible adult at age 2.

So, I say, "I don't know." And my soul smiles. This is a time when I sound like a mess.

The 9:30 am water taxi has just pulled up to Playa Isabel. This marks my day in the way the alarm at 5 am used to. There is no clock here, so I keep time by water taxi.

Which means it's time to walk to town for breakfast.

I still want to know if pelicans make noise.

Coati Mundi

Either you will
go through this door
or you will not go through.
If you go through
there is always the risk
of remembering your name.
Things look at you doubly
and you must look back
and let them happen.
If you do not go through
it is possible
to live worthily
to maintain your attitudes
to hold your position
to die bravely
but much will blind you,
much will evade you,
at what cost who knows?
The door itself
makes no promises.
It is only a door.
~Adrienne Rich

Living without doors, windows and walls has some unexpected perks, for sure. Visitors from geckos to iguanas, birds to badgers come in uninvited, and I can't argue with them or kick them out. In fact, I'm co-habitating with a resident iguana in the rock forming the back "wall" of my home. His name, by the way, is Iggy Pop.

Last night a coati mundi visited my home. This intruder, a large scavenger who looks half an ant-eater and half a large raccoon, woke me out of a deep sleep as he prowled around the kitchen searching for leftover lime rinds. I watched him from the (now not so safe) bed, realizing that mosquito netting is no protection against savage animals scrounging for fruit. But as I watched his futile efforts to find anything to steal, I felt less afraid and more thrilled; who goes on vacation and gets to hang out with a coati mundi?

Knowing that critters will wake me at night gives me strange comfort. Since I'm confident there are no bears or lions prowling the seaside, I go to bed each night with a smile of anticipation, hoping for a break-in rather than wary of one. When I hear my 3 am visitor, I quietly turn on my flashlight to get a better view, and welcome the distraction.

Back at home I may have cursed the noise, the constant wind, the impossibility of sleeping in. At home I would have used a break in to explain why my meditation was interrupted, why I'm not feeling so centered, why my entire day is "off."

Here in Yelapa though, the coati mundi becomes the perfect object for my awareness, and the 3 am visitor decides when I will practice perfect concentration. I finally understand.

Wilderness

*"Thousands of tired, nerve-shaken, over-civilized people are
beginning to find out that going to the mountain top is
going home; that wilderness is a necessity."*
~John Muir

"Be in your body." When I was younger, I thought I
knew what that meant – and for me it was running or
hiking or lifting weights or . . . well anything active. I
didn't realize back then that intention played such a
large role in what effects I could expect.

I had two major intentions in my twenties when it
came to my body. I stayed constantly active to
distract myself away from what my body was truly
feeling. I ran marathons to run away from my pain. I
exercised because I was never truly satisfied with the
way my body looked. At that time, I had no clue I
really had an "inner body" to hang out with and get to
know.

I got into Yoga because I was stiff and getting injured.
I stayed for a very different reason. To make a long
story short, I found out what it really means to be in
my body, truly experiencing (moment by moment)
what my body was experiencing. Watching sensations
rise and subside with my breath. Finding a lovely
place to call home.

I realized that intelligence resides in every cell of my
body. Doing yoga became practice for doing life.

So now, as I walk through the jungle toward the oasis of a cool waterfall, I move to immerse myself in my experience rather than run away from it.

This shift in perspective slows my pace to notice the snake that looks exactly like a vine hanging from a thorny tree, rather than speeding past it.

It allows me to stop and watch a thousand spiders emerge from a hollow log, rather than watching my heart rate.

It means I count macaws in the trees rather than calories.

It means that both my soul and my body have been moved today.

Boats

*"I really don't know why it is that all of us are so
committed to the sea, except I think it's because in addition
to the fact that the sea changes, and the light changes, and
ships change, it's because we all came from the sea. And it
is an interesting biological fact that all of us have in our
veins the exact same percentage of salt in our blood that
exists in the ocean, and, therefore, we have salt in our blood,
in our sweat, in our tears. We are tied to the ocean. And
when we go back to the sea - whether it is to sail or to watch
it - we are going back from whence we came."*
~[Remarks at the Dinner for the America's Cup Crews,
September 14 1962]
~ John F. Kennedy

The ever present and plentiful fishing boats hold my
attention perfectly every day. Most people make their
living here by catching fish, cooking fish, selling fish
or a combination of all three.

In a bay home to bottlenose and spotted dolphins,
humpback whales, marlin, swordfish, giant rays, sting
rays, octopus, jelly fish, and more, I find this simple
act of being in a tiny boat – from a one man kayak on
up -- in that big deep sea courageous.

The fisherman works alone or with one other person.
With a net or a line from a simple reel, they wait
patiently for the fish to come to them.

Frigates, seagulls, cormorants and pelicans hover over some of the boats, hoping to steal their lunch from the fishermen. It's how you can tell if a boat has caught fish.

My scope widens now to notice the sailboats. So beautiful as they saunter into the little bay that is Yelapa. The wind seems perfectly conjured for an elegant entrance. My heart begins to race as I feel this uncontrollable yearning to sail along with them.

Yachts motor in as well. I love that the simple little pueblo of Yelapa is a destination for fancy yachts. They come here to get away from fakery just like I've done.

And the fishermen continue to fish. And wave.

The Path

"I can't be worried about that shit.
Life goes on, man."
~Big Lebowski

The path through town, although literally set in stone, is cobbled and uneven. The width varies, sometimes only wide enough for one person and then opening up again. The path is impeded daily by various elements.

Dogs and cats, sunning themselves, stretch out for me to step over. Piles of wet cement often greet me as I get to the edge of the pueblo. A delivery of eggs or bottled water or cases of beer may show up to block my path.

The four wheelers, the mules, the horse shit and the dog shit (although it gets cleaned up daily) are also present to keep it interesting. The obstacles keep me alert and give me the opportunity to actively engage with my surroundings.

There are natural and daily obstacles here that feel benign and yet when looked at from our antiseptic, totally measured and manicured lifestyles can seem threatening. Back in the U.S., it's easy to check out. We've uniformed everything. We demand smooth highways, even sidewalks, level floors.

We value consistency above all else, confusing this for integrity.

We end up ossifying and become hardened in our need for uniformity. We get rigid and set in our ways. We celebrate those who are the best at being rigidly who they've defined themselves to be because it feels reassuring to go to bed and wake up with exactly the same person.

What is much truer is that we all wake up different. I wake up as a different person than who I was the night before. Last night I finished a book that opened my mind in a way it had never been opened before. Last night no coati mundi woke me. Last night the earth rotated to give me a new and unique relationship with the sun and the moon this morning.

The sky shyly offers another glimpse of herself to me. This morning the tide is low, there are new snails covering the rocks along the shoreline. The current is flowing in a decidedly different direction than it was yesterday.

Today awaits. The cobbled and obstacle-strewn path through the Pueblo invites me to walk with both eyes open, blinders off, guard rails missing, safety measures non-existent.

Salsa Lessons

"I must admit my many inconsistencies. But since I am called 'Mahatma', I might well endorse Emerson's saying that 'Foolish consistency is the hobgoblin of little minds.' There is, I fancy, a method in my inconsistencies. In my opinion, there is a consistency running through my seeming inconsistencies, as in Nature there is unity running through seeming diversity." (YI, 13-2-1930, p52)
~Mahatma Gandi

Everyday at the beach I order salsa. "Salsa Picante" is what I order to differentiate it from pico de gallo. And every day they bring a different salsa. Why? Because every day they take what is available, what is ripe and what is fresh, what is ready and what is PRESENT, and make their salsa picante from scratch.

Yesterday was orange and HOT as hell and so delicious, even if the texture was slightly too runny for my expectations.

Today it is red, green, and white, chunky and crunchy, made from serano chilis, fragrant tomatoes, and onions. So spicy, so chunky and so delicious, even though I missed the specific hot taste of the habanero.

One day they served a salsa that was oily and smoky; I didn't enjoy it the way I had the others, but it was perfect for the "taco de pescado" I was eating and I never would have tried a smoky salsa on my own.

I quickly learned I couldn't rely on getting the salsa I loved; there is no formula except to use what is fresh and what is present. I had to stay open to what showed up.

Because of that, I've now experienced an array of flavors, textures, colors, and burning sensations just by sitting on a beach ordering salsa.

Walking Home

later that night
i held an atlas in my lap
ran my fingers across the whole world
and whispered
where does it hurt?

it answered
everywhere
everywhere
everywhere.
~Warsan Shire

I walk home from dinner in the moonlight, with my trusty headlamp and flashlight, to the sound of the surf crashing right along the rocky path I'm traversing. Many times the waves wash across my feet, which is why the only shoes I wear here are flip flops.

Tonight the ocean is very rough and the sea itself covers the path in certain places. A large piece of driftwood bars my normal route. I take off my shoes to have even more connection to the sandy, gravelly, uncertain way home.

I climb over the driftwood carefully, feeling proud of myself for navigating this treacherous path so gracefully. Before this thought leaves my head, my bare foot slips on a rock.

As I land on my ass and continue to slide toward the sea, I notice I'm laughing. "Pride cometh before the fall" I yell into the abyss.

Now I have a scraped up butt cheek, a bloody foot, and another tangible lesson in life. No matter how careful, how prepared, how confident I am, I will encounter rough seas. I will meet obstructions on my path. I will think I'm totally capable, and then I will fall.

Life will hurt. I may get bloodied; I may feel broken. And then I'll get up and continue home anyway.

Tonight I could live with this inevitability without resisting it. I understood that painful falls on slippery paths doesn't mean I'm ever not whole. Even this hurt has somehow healed another piece of my aching heart. THIS is wholeness.

Beach Dogs

"The animals are more ancient than us; they are our ancient brothers and sisters. They enjoy a seamless presence -- a lyrical unity with the earth. The knowing of the earth is in them. The Zen-like silence and thereness of the landscape is mirrored in the silence and the solitude of animals. Animals know nothing of Freud, Jesus, Buddha, Wall Street, the Pentagon, or the Vatican. They live outside the politics of human intention. Somehow they already inhabit the eternal."
~John O'Donahue

Dog on the beach, lays his head on my lap.
His ear like a blood shot eye
raw, red, torn,
Gazes up at me.
Tears in my eyes, I feel stupid.

I pet him, massage him,
Speak to him in English, then Spanish
Sing to him under cover of my breath.
Tears and wonder . . . who did this to him?
Tears still flowing, I try to hide them.

Why are you petting a beach dog?
Wait, are you crying?
What's your problem?
Dog on the beach runs off.
I want to run too.

Stairs

"The mind's subconscious physical memory was so powerful, so adroit in its calculations, that climbing only two or three stairs set the formula. When a step of a slightly different measure was encountered, a person was sure to stumble over that fraction of space not recognized by the body's swift memory."
~Sarah Stonich, *These Granite Islands*

Here in Mexico stairs have their own personality. The stairs I walk daily to and from the beach (a la playa) require my full attention. I've started to get to know each step and have even named a few of them. One is tall and wide, another only half covered with cement, one side higher than the other. The next step is so short my toes hang off it, and the next step shallow enough to have me teetering precariously for a moment. The next step feels deep in comparison. As though I'm stepping into an abyss. Then the stair seems to rise up and meet my bare foot, reassuring my body that it was there all along.

Each stair offers itself up to me to be known and seen and understood. Each step requires my full presence. The stairwell, a mish mash of personalities, the very opposite of "formula," keeps my mind checked in.

This to me is the perfect walking meditation. Perfectly manicured zen gardens, fabricated labyrinths, and expansive parkways pale in comparison.

Love List

I've been thinking so much about my friend Missy and her habit of going to bars. Missy felt compelled to take a journal to bars by herself on a regular basis. She'd pick a spot where she could observe people, order a beer, and write down everything she loved about everyone she saw. Her life experience was based on an intention that generated ease in the world, thus her habit produced joy.

Missy was an angel, and was not meant long for this world. She never accumulated much, going where her spirit led her without any agenda or need for an outcome. So when Missy was asked by her dying friend to become a surrogate mother to her children, she said yes without hesitation. After letting go of all her possessions, she started her drive across the country to answer the call of her soul. She was killed in a car accident on her way there.

While her story seems tragic, Missy "got it" and really had nothing else to learn from this lifetime. Her life was an example of equanimity and individuality. She stood out because she didn't care about standing out or about fitting in.

Anywhere she was led, including death, was perfectly fine with her. Had she made it to Georgia to be the mom she agreed to be, she would have sourced that life experience from the same place she always had: from presence, moment to moment awareness, and a powerful lack of pretense.

There are many people like Missy here. I admire so many people and am learning so much from them, but have not yet established deep bonds of friendship. The language barrier and cultural differences make the process slower. So it does get lonely sometimes.

While I no longer believe in the American dream and now know I can live abroad without boredom, without hardship, without missing things, I still really do miss miss my boys, my friends, my family. If only I could bring my loved ones to Yelapa with me!

Because I miss so many people, and because Missy has been on my mind, I started a love list (a list of all the people I love). I write names on the list all day long, whenever I think of someone I love. I'm amazed to find out how often my loved ones are on my mind.

Mexico inspires me to be more loving, encourages me to break down the walls around my heart, and requires nothing more than receptivity. My love list will soon require another notebook.

Both/And

*"So this is my life. And I want you to know that I am both
happy and sad and I'm still trying to figure out how that
could be."*
~ Stephen Chbosky, *The Perks of Being a Wallflower*

I know that when I go back to the states I will
unwittingly buy into that dangerous game of
either/or. I'll allow myself to be pigeon-holed, sorted
and labeled.
I'll be made to feel guilty; ashamed for feeling
"negative" emotions like grief, depression, sadness,
anger, or horror.

Here, it feels entirely possible that we as humans are
capable of feeling all the feelings. Here I witness my
capacity to hold a myriad of emotions quite gracefully.
All at once. And I want to cultivate that part of me
that can hold it all and feel it all. I am afraid of losing
this feeling when I return. It makes me not want to
return.

Feeling happy and sad at the same time, peaceful and
wild at the same time, makes sense when I am here. I
need this to keep making sense.

There is peaceful.
There is wild.
I am both at the same time.
~sum

Self Help

It's fucked up how people get judged for being real,
and how people get loved for being fake.
 ~Tupac

Today I started crying, watching the guys on the
beach selling their wares. My favorite is Bollio.
"Shopping Tine" he yells, and laughs when a
customer offers him an embarrassing amount for his
product. "Free joint when you buy sun teen!"
"Cheaper than Wal-Mart!" I love this man.

This culture is a whole new world in some ways. I've
learned so much from the people of this village.
People don't spend any time trying to define who they
are. They aren't trying to be "better" or "more" or
"spiritual." They are complex in their simplicity.
There's no guile; no need to pretend they are someone
else. No need to put oneself in a box to be just one
small part of the amazing humans they are.

I spent most of my life believing I needed to better
myself. Change myself. Improve myself. Then I
started paying attention to when I feel the most at
ease in my body and the people I am the most relaxed
around. I'm drawn to people who are easy on
themselves and others. Who don't question their
worthiness, have nothing to do with the yoga
industrial complex, have never bought one self-help
book.

I'm not super comfy around yoga people, or self help crowds, or people who are self proclaimed healers, gurus, and light bearers.

I'd rather be on the beach with a good book and a nice shot of tequila, a cigar and some good music, than attend another superiority seminar masked as "help."

I'm good. You're good. I don't need help being myself. I am myself. And I love the energy surrounding people who are themselves.

Don't worship a bearded man in the sky, or a graven image in a book. Worship the in-breath and the out-breath, the winter breeze caressing your face, the morning rush on the Underground, the simple feeling of being alive, never knowing what is to come. See God in the eyes of a stranger, Heaven in the broken and the ordinary. Worship the ground on which you stand. Make each day a dance, with tears in your eyes, as you behold the divine in every moment, see the absolute in all things relative, and let them call you crazy. Let them laugh and point. You are a yogi of traffic jams and discarded apple cores, aloneness and impossibly blue winter skies, a yogi of broken dreams, mad with truth and devotion and inexplicable joy, and you cannot be saved now.
~Jeff Foster

Enough

This is the doctrine of my religion.
Place your hands
into soil to feel
grounded.
Wade in
water to feel
emotionally
healed.
Fill your
lungs with fresh
air to feel
mentally clear.
Raise your face
To the heat of the sun
and connect with
that fire to feel
your own immense
power.
~Victoria Erickson

I have a friend visiting, so we hired a boat to visit the town of Chimo today. As we approached the shore, an old--and I do mean old--man in a dinghy met us in the bay to row us to shore.

Once our feet met the sand, we trekked across fish nets to get to the one restaurant in town. Our drink options include--only--bottled water, Coronas, and raicilla (local moonshine made from agave).

For food they offer--only--ceviche, lobster, and whatever fish the fishermen bring in. Condiments consist of limes, salt, and hot sauce.

We order, and as we down our cerveza, we gaze out at the sea.

There is no internet, cell phones don't have service, and even electricity is limited. They don't speak English. Dogs and cats run in and out of the place, which is basically a palapa with a sand floor.

Horses, mules, and donkeys congregate on the path. A little boy runs up and begins playing with a horse. He's having a grand adventure with a horse; there's nothing else more impressive to steal his attention.

Mexico has my heart. My goals have changed. At the top of my goals list are: "learn to speak Spanish," "find a way to bring Finn (my dog) to Mexico," and "simplify life even more."

This is more than enough.

Dominoes

"Let go of certainty. The opposite isn't uncertainty. It's openness, curiosity and a willingness to embrace paradox, rather than choose up sides. The ultimate challenge is to accept ourselves exactly as we are, but never stop trying to learn and grow."
~Tony Schwartz

I played dominoes with people I've met here tonight. At one point I realized that my entire reality crashed like a string of dominos on my 50th birthday. At first I tried to set all the dominoes back up, guarding the string with my life. But there's not really a way to keep a string of dominos from eventually falling again. They are, by nature, meant to crash.

Now, I'm just beginning to understand that I'm not meant to rebuild anything. My new space and role is to simply be.

My new to do list is to be as much myself as possible. To self-sustain. To live through this massive ending to everything I built and was in the world. To experience death. Finality. And to truly get that I am not meant to go down with the fall of those dominos.

I exist independently of the game.

Still

No more multi tasking.
No more availability at all hours for all people
No more care taking.

No desire to be the boss, take charge, push.
No belief that I'm a leader in the community.
No need to run myself ragged.

Still want to do good.
Live quietly.
Pet my dog.

Still captivated by the birds.

Still enamored of the elegant trogon
Dazzled by the Yellow Grosbeak
Admonished by the West Mexican Chackalaca.

Still impressed by the Boat billed fly catcher
Inspired by the Magnificent Frigate
Curious about Cormorants and Gulls.

Still chasing blue footed boobies
Watching Wood storks
Fearing turkey Vultures

Still excited about White Herons
Following blue cranes
Frolicking with snowy egrets.

Still wondering if Pelicans speak.

Yoga

The impulse to stretch is built into the very pulse of life: it is
the expansive moment, before the contraction, the filling
before the emptying, the charge before the discharge. It is the
child's arms reaching for its mother, or the lover embracing
her love. It is the legs stepping out into a walk, then a run.
It is the propensity to go beyond where you have been, and
once you have found comfort in that new place, to wriggle
and move beyond that too. It is the wrapping of the heart
around more, and the broadening of the mind past its own
limits. Stretching will always have its place, and from the
infinite creative potential it expresses,
we will continually unfold.
~Gil Hedley

Yoga in the jungle. Under the trees. Stopping to watch
the coati mundis and listen to the chichilacas. So
different from what I've known.

I don't know when I'll get back to teaching. I need
time off from anything and everything like that. I've
been hurt by the spiritual community. Betrayed by
new age enlightened people and it has left a really bad
taste in my mouth. I need to revisit how I show up in
what has become the yoga industrial complex. Right
now my yoga practice consists of being alone. I'm not
trying to be a better person or a leader of my
community. This is the yoga of realizing myself.

And I need to forget.

Sacred

"I have learned that to be with those I like is enough."
~Walt Whitman

"Semana Santa," the week before Easter, is devoted to the sacred. As I get to be a spectator this week, I'm so struck by how important family is here.

Dads hugging their little girls, moms being cared for by their sons, abuelos y abuelas swimming in the ocean alongside the niños. They sense they belong to each other and are made larger in each others' attentions.

It seems at first to squelch unique expression; but no one cares to establish their unique specialness apart from their family.

Our culture seems so foreign here. The need to stand out and stand apart and be superior is simply absent here.

The ease with which they show love and tactile presence here is astounding. It keeps bringing tears to my eyes.

Their presence with each other is what makes this week sacred.

Healing

expansive heart,
may you rest easy and trust

sensation-filled body,
may you stay courageous and feel

trusting mind,
may you talk yourself into all of it

royal and sacred soul,
may you lead us all.

Rebirth

"When tears come, I breathe deeply and rest. I know I am
swimming in a hallowed stream where many have gone
before. I am not alone, crazy, or having a nervous
breakdown. . . My heart is at work, my soul is awake."
~ Mary Margaret Funk

Yesterday I cried all day. For so many reasons, I cried,
grieved, felt broken in two. I've been through the
ringer. Especially in the past 9 months. Yesterday was
the 9 month mark since my fiftieth birthday and the
events that led to the fuckery.

Yesterday was also my brother Mark's birthday. Only
he died of cancer 16 years ago.

Yesterday I also moved to a different place, away from
people I've grown to love as family. Fatima,
Rodolpho, Flor, Fabiola, Franco, César, Hector, Ismael,
Bollio, René, Juan, Duelma, and Miguel-Angel. I
chickened out and couldn't say goodbye to them
because I couldn't stop sobbing just thinking about it.

Today I know the tears were a sort of rebirth -
preceded by a nine month gestation - and that this
person I am now is not at all the person I was 9
months ago.

Today is a new day. The fact that it is Easter isn't lost
on me. I'm 50 and I'm just barely becoming me again.

I believe we all become who we are until the very day we die.

I feel more carefree and childlike than I did when I was twenty.

I feel less certain and more raw than I've ever felt.

This is me today.

I'm still broken. I don't know how long it will take to feel whole again. But because of Yelapa I have the courage to stay broken open.

To stay alive and awake and aware and tender in the face of this tremendous, beyond-ability-to-comprehend life.

I believe in myself again.

I believe in my dignity.

I believe that I'm going to have an exciting, bittersweet, joyful adventure and, for those of you who've witnessed a little taste of this chapter of my life, I feel honored and humbled, astonished and thankful you've been willing to join me.

"When I stand before thee at the day's end, thou shalt see my scars and know
that I had my wounds and also my healing."
~Rabindranath Tagore

Dad

"Few delights can equal the mere presence of one whom we trust utterly."
~George MacDonald

I'm back in Utah. I sat outside all morning with my dad and my dog, in the shade of the aspen tree where I always feel my brother's presence.

My dad and I are as different as two people could possibly be. For a while I tried to reject him. Then this whole thing happened, where my "spiritual family" made it clear that they were rejecting me. Somehow my dad found out about it, insisted I come over, and suddenly it was the only place I wanted to be. At home with my dad. In the arms of my father.

Months later I went to Mexico and noticed how the Mexican people love and respect their families, their elders, their children. I sat there on the beach having a huge "aha" moment. I do NOT need my dad to agree with me. But I DO need my dad.

Today, as I carried my coffee with me into his back yard, silently marveling over the glimmering leaves of the aspen tree, my dad said "I always loved the smell of coffee." I can't really explain why that simple sentence meant so much to me, but it was his way of saying he accepts me the way I am.

Return to Return

"There is no doubt you're in my heart now."
~Guns and Roses (Patience)

I'm in Utah for six more days. I've lived here for 18 years. Longer than I've lived in one state in my entire life. I have sold my businesses and my house, given away 95% of my possessions, raised my boys and sent them out of state for college. In short, I have no ties left. Except for all of the people I got to know here. You all hold pieces of my heart. And I will miss you. Terribly and certainly, I will miss you. But I'm headed back to Mexico, where my heart even beats differently.

"In those moments when life's hurts tear into the hidden places of your soul, I invite you to enter the refuge of beauty, blessing, our lost mode of prayer and the deep wisdom that each rests upon. It is here that you may find meaning in the unexplained, and the strength that guides you to the close of another day."
~ Gregg Braden, *Secrets of the Lost Mode of Prayer*

Made in the USA
Coppell, TX
07 March 2022

74626878R00049